this 3D book belongs to:

Stereographer	**David E. Klutho**
Designer	**Kirsten Sorton**
3D Graphics Designer	**ron labbe, studio 3D**
3D Photography Assistant	**Jake Huber**
Photo Editor	**Marguerite Schropp Lucarelli**
Writer	**Jeremy Repanich**
Copy Editor	**Megan Collins**
Reporter	**Ryan Hatch**

This 3D book is dedicated to the 3A's – **A**ustin, **A**lly, and **A**aron

Special thanks: Victor and Joan Klutho, John A. Kilo, Laura Henning-Vandeven, Keippi and Dexter Cobble, Bob Chandler and Bigfoot, John Force Racing, Paula Coony, Danica Patrick, Joe Crowley, Regan Schaar, Tod Olson-Weston, Nancy Olson, Masuji Suto, Monty and Jill Perrigo, Nikon USA, Fujifilm Global, Panasonic Lumix 3D, Sony 3D, and Laciny Brothers

SPORTS ILLUSTRATED KIDS

Managing Editor Bob Der

Creative Director Beth Bugler

Assistant Managing Editor Andrea Woo

Imaging Geoffrey Michaud, Dan Larkin, Robert M. Thompson

TIME HOME ENTERTAINMENT
Publisher Jim Childs
Vice President, Brand & Digital Strategy Steven Sandonato
Executive Director, Marketing Services Carol Pittard
Executive Director, Retail & Special Sales Tom Mifsud
Executive Publishing Director Joy Butts
Director, Bookazine Development & Marketing Laura Adam
Finance Director Glenn Buonocore
Associate Publishing Director Megan Pearlman
Assistant General Counsel Helen Wan
Assistant Director, Special Sales Ilene Schreider
Senior Book Production Manager Susan Chodakiewicz
Design & Prepress Manager Anne-Michelle Gallero
Brand Manager Jonathan White
Associate Prepress Manager Alex Voznesenskiy
Assistant Brand Manager Stephanie Braga

Editorial Director Stephen Koepp

Special thanks: Katherine Barnet, Jeremy Biloon, Rose Cirrincione, Jacqueline Fitzgerald, Christine Font, Jenna Goldberg, Hillary Hirsch, David Kahn, Amy Mangus, Kimberly Marshall, Amy Migliaccio, Nina Mistry, Dave Rozzelle, Ricardo Santiago, Adriana Tierno, Vanessa Wu

ISBN 10: 1-61893-078-8
ISBN 13: 978-1-61893-078-1
Library of Congress Control Number: 2013935641
SPORTS ILLUSTRATED KIDS is a trademark of Time Inc.
We welcome your comments and suggestions about SPORTS ILLUSTRATED KIDS Books.
Please write to us at:
    Sports Illustrated Kids Books
    Attention: Book Editors
    P.O. Box 11016
    Des Moines, IA 50336-1016
If you would like to order any of our hardcover Collector's Edition books, please call us at 1-800-327-6388 (Monday through Friday, 7 a.m. to 8 p.m., or Saturday, 7 a.m. to 6 p.m., central time).

Ladies and Gentlemen...

START YOUR GLASSES!

NASCAR
Racing Star
DANICA PATRICK

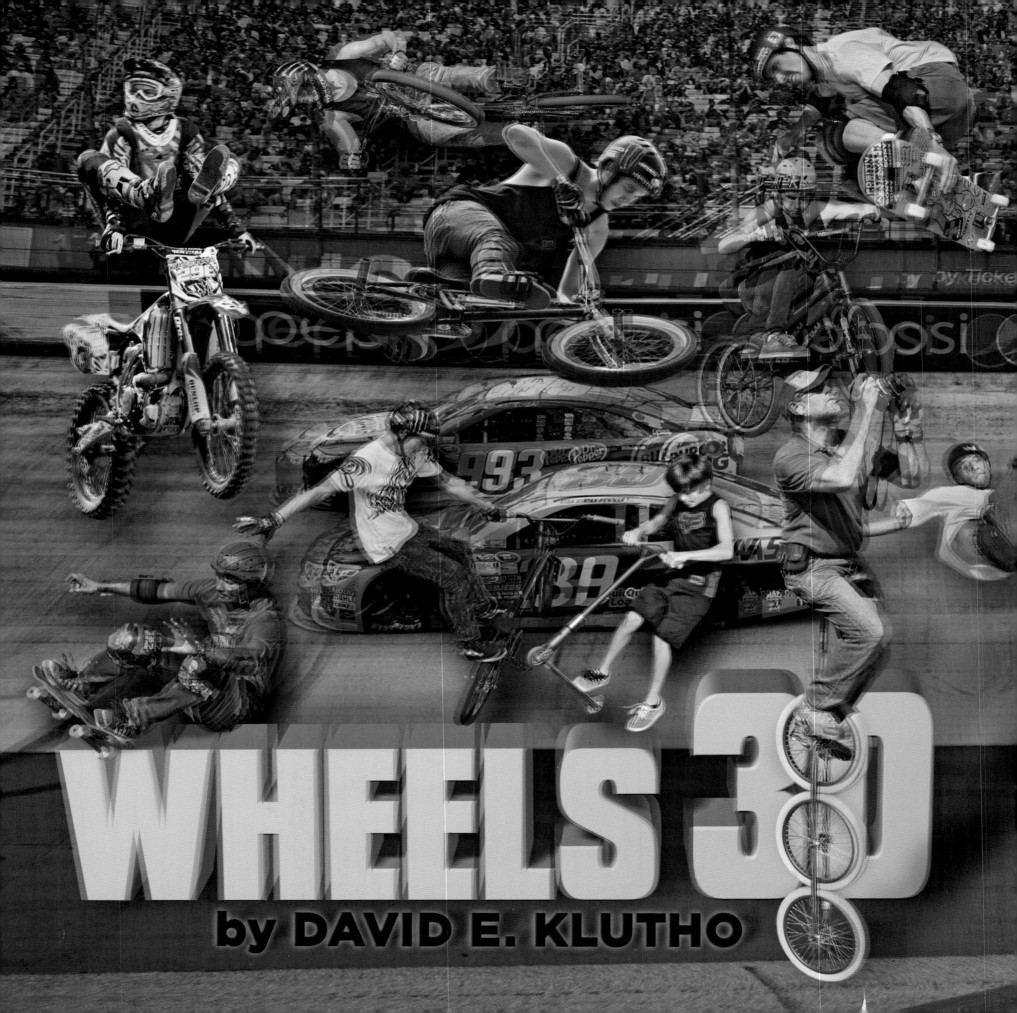

WHEELS 3D

by DAVID E. KLUTHO

Rolling FOREWORD

with Tom Schaar

It's an amazing thing, 3D coming at you. Speeding cars, crushing monster trucks, jumping BMX bikes, sliding motorcycles, and, of course, skateboarders, like me, flying right off the page.

I first got on a skateboard when I was just 3 years old. Now at the age of 13, I'm a professional. I have always surprised myself as to what I can accomplish on the four small wheels attached to my board. I am the youngest competitor to spin a 900 (two and a half rotations in the air), the first-ever person of any age to spin a 1080 (three full rotations), and the youngest rider to win an X Games gold medal.

With all that experience, I've been photographed a lot, and having my picture taken in 3D for this book showed me how different it is. The photographer, David E. Klutho, showed up with double lenses on his cameras and said he was going to shoot from a specific angle to make me able to jump out at you, as you can see in the photo on this page!

This SI KIDS 3D book is loaded with awesome action sports using 3D photography. It is the first-ever 3D book showing a huge variety of wheeled action sports. So here we go — turn the page, tighten your helmet, and prepare to be amazed!

Tschaar

WHEELS 3D

CONTENTS

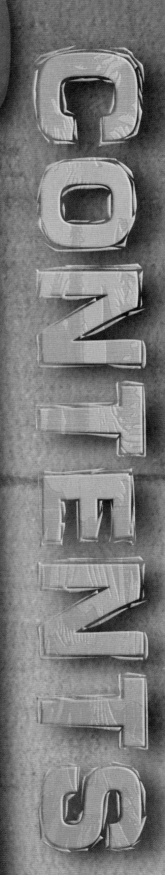

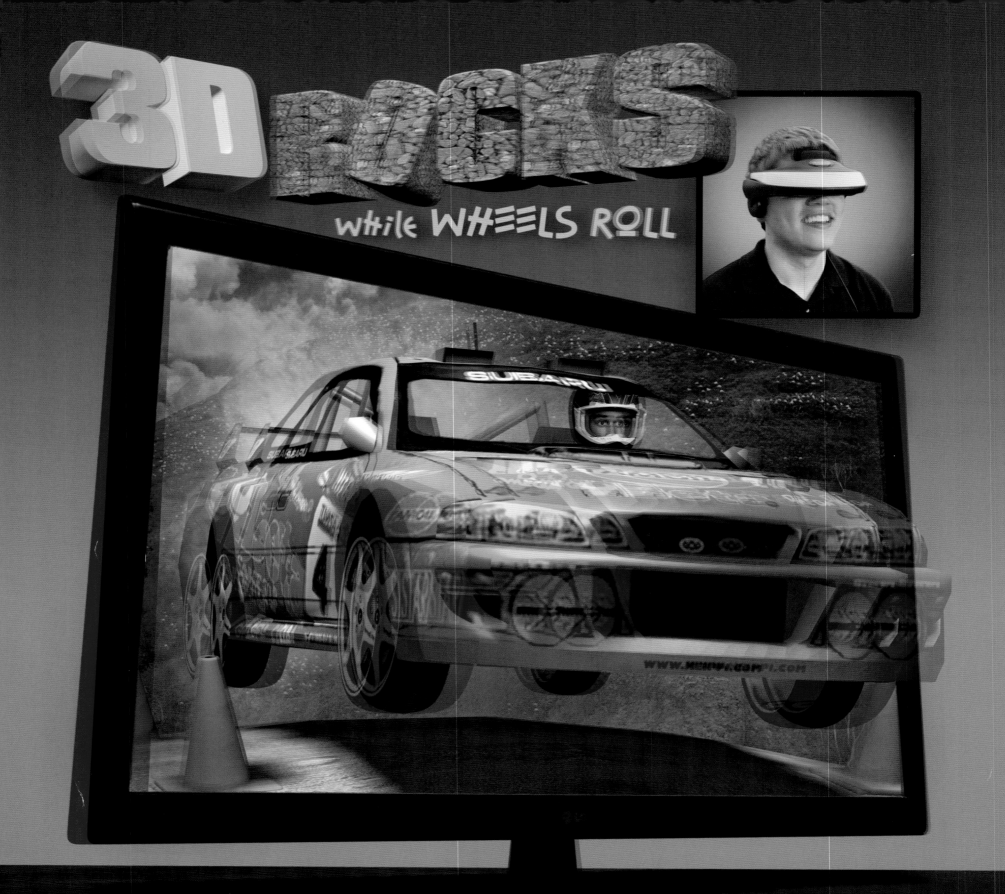

3D ROCKS

while WHEELS ROLL

New technology makes 3D even better in movies, games, education, surgery, architecture — and books! The digital revolution brings stereoscopic vision to almost every aspect of our lives. Real life is in 3D because of our two eyes, and this special ability (known as "stereopsis") helps us appreciate and enjoy the spaces around us. Three dimensions are definitely better than two!

the shades

To play 3D games, you can use a 3D TV or a special headset *(left, inset)* that makes the experience totally immersive. There are two kinds of 3D TVs. One uses battery-powered "active" lenses in the glasses, the other uses polarized "passive" lenses (which Billy is wearing here), just like the ones used at 3D movies.

For this book, you're using "anaglyph" (red and cyan) glasses. Stereoscopic (3D) pictures are actually two slightly different images, one seen by the left eye and one by the right. In the anaglyph process, the two images are color-coded so they can work on a printed page.

In gaming there are 3D systems (like the Nintendo 3DS) that are "autostereoscopic" and don't need any glasses, but they're currently for single users only. Who knows what the future holds for 3D viewing?

— *ron labbe,*
studio 3D

Bottom line: 3D is fun, no matter how you look at it!

Quick Change

In NASCAR, every second counts — and not just while racing on the track. Drivers rely on their crew to make quick pit stops to refuel, get new tires, or fix the car. A six-man crew can make a lightning-fast pit stop, changing four 24-pound tires in as little as 13 seconds.

Inspection Time

A driver and his crew will look for any advantage possible to beat the field. NASCAR rigorously inspects all the cars before and after every race to ensure that competitions are about the best drivers and not the best cars. Here, Nationwide Series driver Timmy Hill's car is closely inspected. Among the details that officials check for is an aerodynamic advantage *(above, right)*. Inspectors use templates to check that the car's shape conforms to regulations. Thanks to a new laser measuring process, tweaks to the bottom of the car that violate the rules can be detected up to 1/1,000th of an inch. Inspectors also look under the hood to check for engine violations. In 2009 one driver was fined for his engine being only .17 inches too big!

The crew for Marcos Ambrose (9)
works hard to keep him on the track.

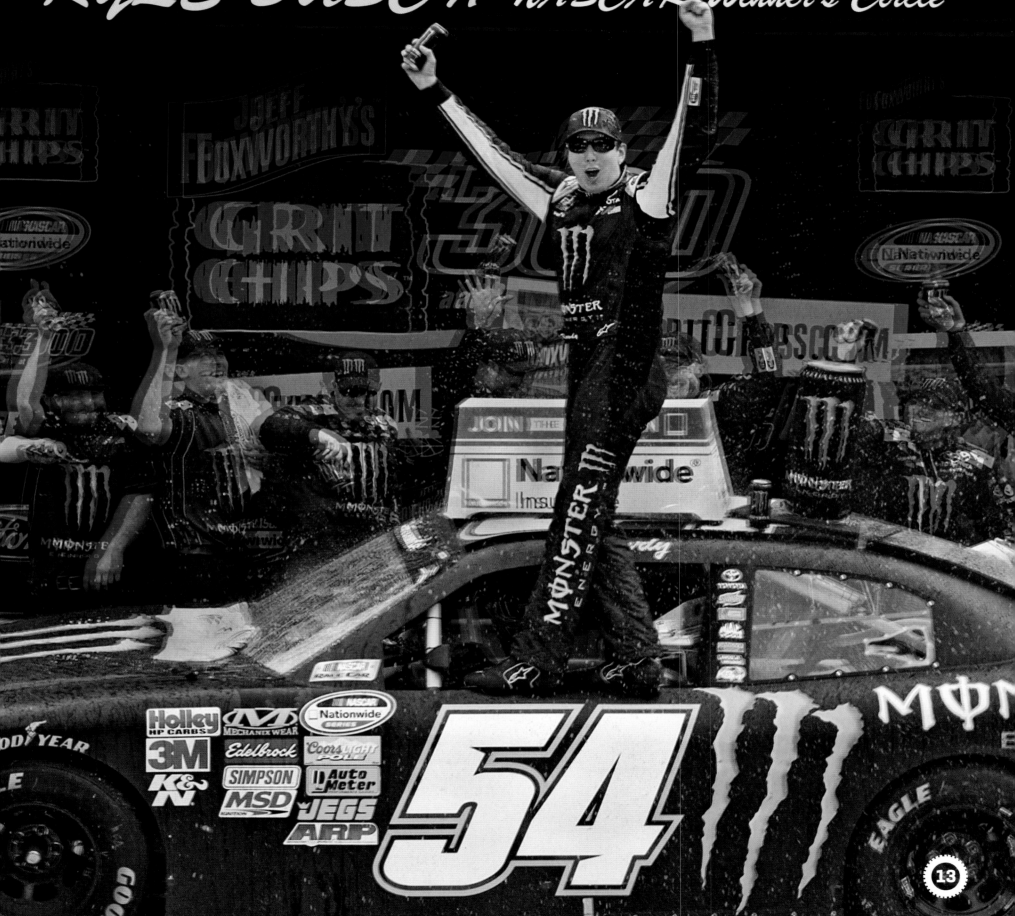

KYLE BUSCH NASCAR Winner's Circle

13

DRIVING FORCE

A Force to Be Reckoned With

In the National Hot Rod Association (NHRA), John Force Racing is the most successful team. John has won 15 series championships, including 10 straight from 1993 to 2002. There are also three other drivers in Force Racing: 2009 series champ Robert Hight, 2012 rookie of the year Courtney Force, and top-fuel dragster racer Brittany Force. When they show up to an event, they show up in full force, with 13 trailers to support four teams. Each team brings two cars and eight motors assembled, ready to race. They also have 65 crew members in tow.

John Force
RACING

Prepare to Win

To build each of these cars, which are worth up to $250,000, it takes 320 hours of labor from start to finish.

Racing is in the genes for Courtney Force of John Force Racing.

A Family Affair

The Force family may have John, the 15-time NHRA Funny Car champ, at its head, but daughter Courtney is in the driver's seat. In 2012, she won the series' rookie of the year award at age 24. She also became the third woman in Funny Car history to win a race. The first? Her sister Ashley in 2008. Another sister, Brittany, races top fuel dragsters.

ROBERT HIGHT

Mr. President

Hight isn't just a great driver, he's the boss. The 2009 NHRA Funny Car season champ is the hands-on president of John Force Racing. "He started here as a mechanic and has done basically every position," says John Force Racing general manager Jason Sharp. "He has a wealth of knowledge on cars." Hight *(right, center)* uses that know-how to tune the cars to perfection. "He told one of the fabricators in the shop, 'If you move that throttle back a quarter of an inch, it would make all the difference in the world.' To you or me, we'd say, 'Really, a quarter of an inch?'" Sharp says. It's that attention to detail and teamwork that is key to JFR's success.

THE CREWS

Each of the four cars has its own expert crew

Tuned to Perfection

The work on the car doesn't stop once it rolls out of the shop. Crews monitor and tune it extensively at the track, too. Between runs, Hight's crew jumps into action to service the car. They have just 55 minutes to take the motor apart to inspect and repair it. "It's a controlled chaos," Sharp says. "On more senior teams, crew members can do it with their eyes closed." Throughout the car, 40 sensors monitor its performance, giving the crew important feedback on where to focus their efforts. Sometimes they even need gas masks to do their job. When the crew test-fires the engine in the pit, they require protection from the nitromethane fuel that powers the car.

Burning Rubber

After the car is built, the crew carefully calibrates the engine, and the track is scouted — it's finally time to race. A series event takes three days, and its winner is determined by a 16-team match-race tournament, which has its seeding set by qualifying times. The cars fly down the 1,000-foot straightaways at speeds approaching 320 miles per hour.

Demolition Men

At state fairs and monster truck rallies, you can find cars speeding around that aren't racing. In demolition derby, the cars ram into each other as hard as they can, trying to destroy one another. The last one standing is the winner.

Winning Rally

NASCAR drivers may think that speeding around banked oval tracks is tough, but it's no match for what Rally Car racers endure. Drivers have to ride on asphalt, dirt, packed ice, mud, and even giant puddles. These souped-up production cars are turbocharged to go from zero to 60 miles per hour in three seconds and can reach speeds near 140 miles per hour. Their races are usually broken into mini-races called stages. And the driver isn't alone in the car — he's got a navigator onboard (called a co-driver) to help strategically guide him through the course.

Winging It

As sprint car drivers whip around the dirt track at speeds up to 140 miles per hour, two signature wings keep these powerful cars from going airborne. The cars can generate up to 900 horsepower, but weigh only 1,200 pounds. With that much power, they could easily flip without the huge wings that sit on top and in front of the car. Instead of helping the car lift off, the wings hold the car down and keep it on the track.

BIKes

This is no Tour de France. BMX cyclists aren't about pedaling for miles and flying down the road as efficiently as possible. Most of the time, BMXers are focused on riding with style. You'll see them in skate parks inside giant tubes (like this one in Portland, Oregon), on vert ramps in the X Games, or flying around empty swimming pools in Los Angeles. When they race, they conquer off-road courses, which require them to navigate dirt jumps in a crowded field of BMXers.

> "I have always loved BMX and I always will. Trends come and go, attitudes change like the direction of the wind, but my love for my bike never will. I think back to when I was 10 years old and I would borrow a friend's bike and jump off of curbs. I still get that same feeling of sheer excitement when I've made the bike go up high in the air."

Jamie Bestwick

BMX Racing

In 2008, BMX racing made its debut as an official Olympic sport at the Beijing Games. But you don't need to be a gold-medal contender to get yourself into a race now. USA BMX encourages participation at all levels, dividing competitions by age, gender, and skill level.

Collin Schmidt is moving up the amateur ranks of BMX racing.

1 2 3 4 5
8 6
7

tHE
COUNT
DOUBLECROSS
FaCtORY RIDER
COLLIN SCHMIDt

Balancing Act

As if riding a unicycle weren't hard enough, Eli, a 12-year-old unicyclist, likes to up the level of difficulty. First, he rides a unicycle with a smaller wheel, which makes it tougher to go fast. Second, he can ride while juggling scooter and skateboard wheels!

TOXIC

This 10,000-pound monster truck is certainly harmful to the health of any car that gets in its way on the Monster Nation tour. Toxic, owned by three brothers in Western New York, first hit the scene in 2010. Topped with a Ford Super-Duty body, Toxic is 11 feet tall and nearly 13 feet wide, boasting 1,500 horsepower. The truck was built by Patrick Enterprises, which has created more than 100 trucks in competition, including Bigfoot, Grave Digger, and Dan Patrick's own monster truck, Samson.

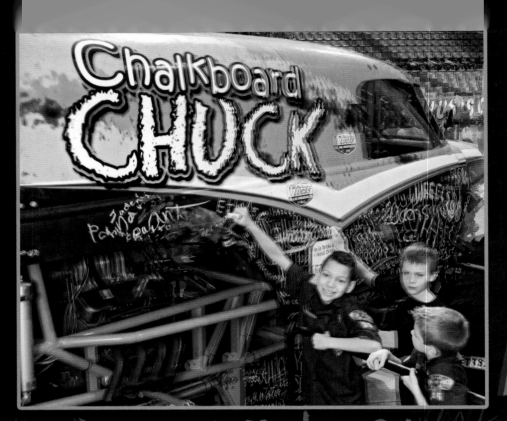

Mini Me
Not all trucks have to be monster-sized. Small radio-control cars are a fun hobby for all ages.

Tired Out

Crew members for the monster truck Predator install terra tires that weigh about 900 pounds and stand 66 inches tall and 43 inches wide. Their job is made a lot easier by a remote control jack, which turns this Herculean effort into a one-man-job.

Monster Mission

Monty Perrigo of Columbia, Missouri, builds custom monster trucks. He turned this old military transport vehicle into a truck that's an ode to U.S. troops.

Smashing Success

Basketball has Dr. James Naismith, NASCAR has Bill France Sr., and monster trucks has Bob Chandler. In the late 1970s, Chandler *(right)* invented the sport when he turned a Ford F250 pickup truck into a behemoth. In 1981, he smashed his first car, and crowds couldn't get enough. Eventually, as more monster trucks came on the scene, they weren't just putting on exhibitions, they were racing. While there are many trucks out there, the most famous is Bigfoot. And the biggest Bigfoot? Bigfoot 5 *(right)*, which features 10-foot-tall tires.

One Giant Leap . . .

In 1999, Dan Runte set a Guinness World Record when he drove Bigfoot 14 off a ramp, sending it sailing 202 feet. Thirteen years later, with his record having been broken, Runte came to the 4-Wheel Jamboree Nationals in Indianapolis, Indiana, to reclaim the mark. Below is Bigfoot 18 soaring 214 feet, eight inches to shatter the previous record of 208 feet.

Bigfoot 15, driven by
Darron Schnell

NAKED MONSTER

Looking under
the hood of
Bigfoot 18

Equalizer, driven by
Mike Hawkins

TailGator, driven by
Doug Noelke

MONSTER KIDS

SIR CRUSHALOT vs. KID KJ

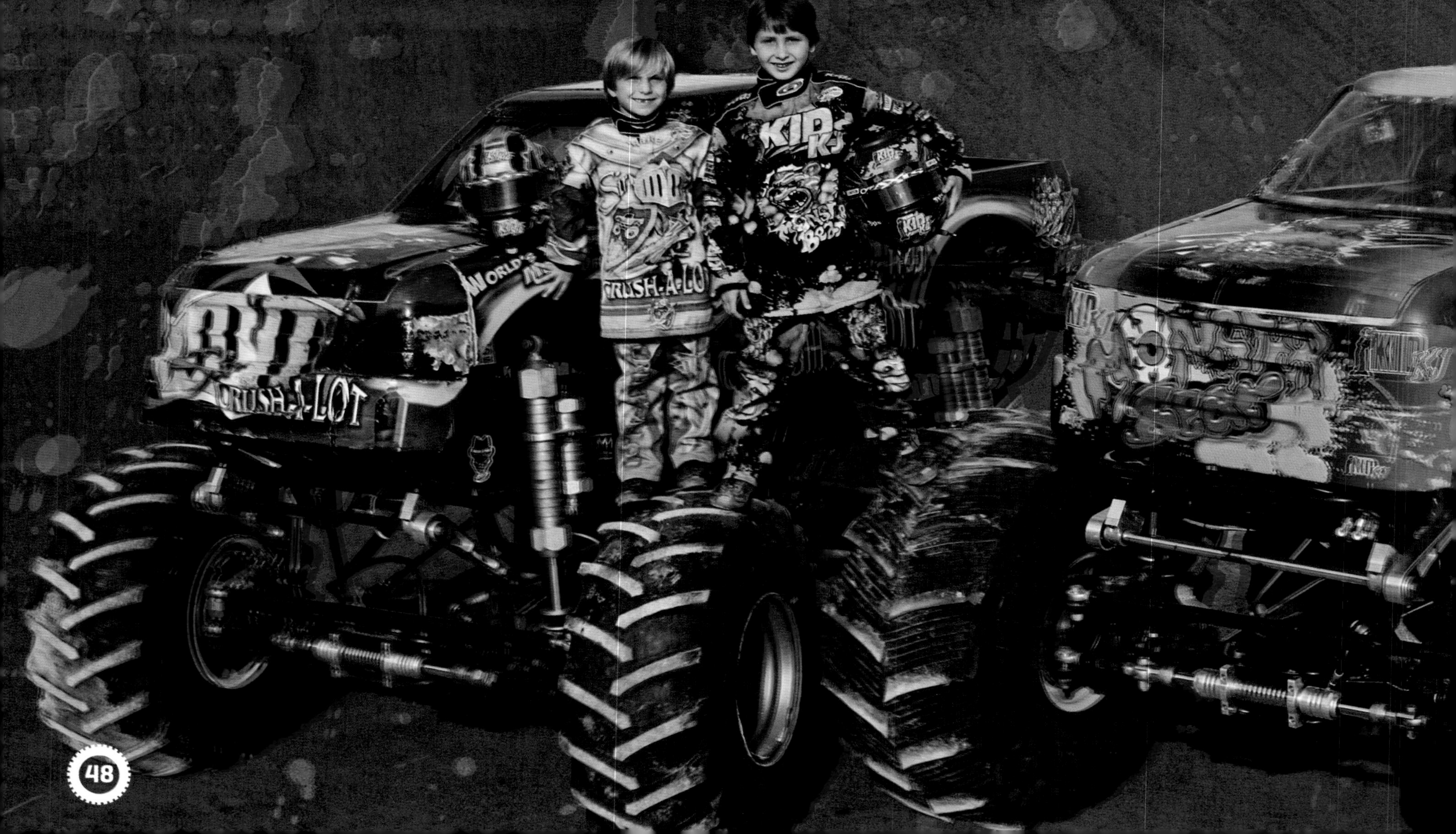

JUST LIKE THE BIG GUYS

Before Kaid Jaret Olson-Weston — who is known as Kid KJ — came around, kids weren't racing monster trucks. "I went to a monster truck show when I was 3, and I loved it so much that I told my mom and dad that I wanted one right away," he says. Unfortunately, a truck his size didn't exist, and his parents' first attempt to get him a ride didn't do the trick. "They bought me a monster truck go-kart, and I told them, 'That's not a real one.'" So his parents, both monster truck drivers, found a custom builder to create a truck fit for a kid. Instead of a 16-foot-tall truck, Kid KJ has one half the size, at eight feet. He started out driving in an exhibition during monster truck rallies — doing wheelies and crushing a little yellow school bus made of Styrofoam. Now the 10-year-old drives against other kids, including his 8-year-old brother, Jake. They speed around ovals, go over jumps, drive over cars, and do tricks at about 100 events each year.

KJ (left) and Jake work on KJ's truck.

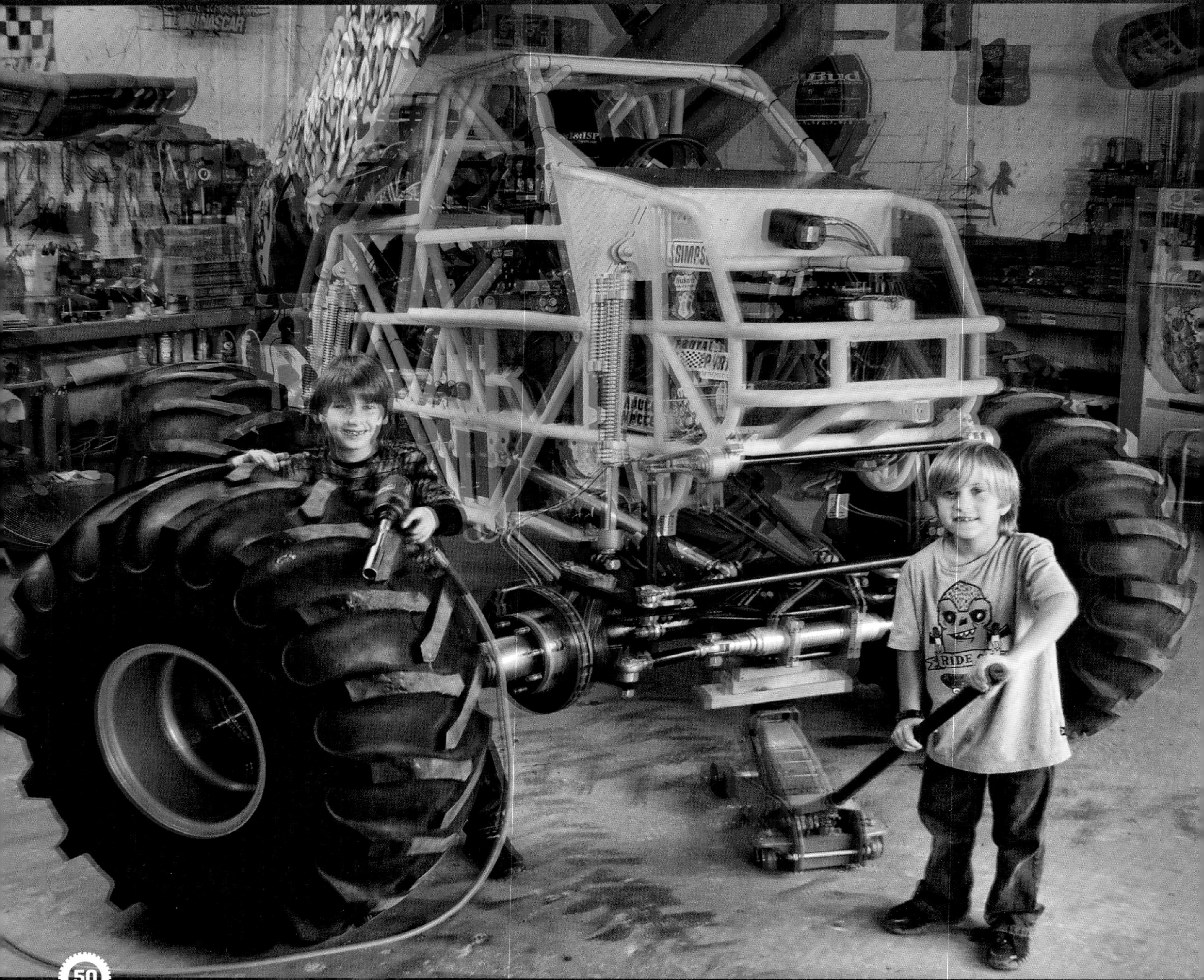

Splashdown!

Even though they can spend up to 14 hours a day working on their trucks and travel all around the country to drive, KJ and Jake still choose to play with cars during their free time. "We drive our [radio-control] cars a lot," KJ says, showing off his improvised jump-making skills by sailing his truck over the pool.

Support System

Drag races don't just happen on smooth expanses of
pavement, they happen deep in the mud, too.
Supercharged four-wheel-drive trucks with jacked-up
suspension and big tractor tires compete against each
other in soupy mud pits. The wheelie bar pictured here
gives the truck stability. If the truck pops a wheelie, the
bar will prevent it from rolling over backward.

MOTORCYCLES

Mud Sport

Every summer since 1972, the best off-road motorcyclists in the country have competed on dirt tracks all over the U.S. to crown the AMA champion in three divisions: 450cc, 250cc, and women's MX. The 450 and 250 refer to the size of the motorcycle's engine. The bigger the number, the more powerful the bike. The riders fly over huge jumps, crash in big muddy ruts, and negotiate hairpin turns at 12 different events. Kids on minibikes *(below)* also get into the action!

The *Wheelie Wizzard*

Tyler Shepard

Shepard is known more for his style than his speed. Calling himself the **Wheelie Wizzard**, Shepard pops crazy wheelies at events across the country. He became inspired to perform his tricks when as a kid growing up in Ohio, he saw a show by Doug Domokos, "The Wheelie King." Now Shepard is the one wowing crowds. He brings three to four bikes to his shows, including an electric bike with no front wheel, and the minibike (*above*), which can eject its wheel. Shepard isn't just playing in the dirt out there, he also shows amazing balance by riding on his back wheel along two-by-four wood planks.

ICE RACING

Slippery Situation

Riders in the Extreme International Ice Racing tour accelerate on bikes that can go from zero to 60 miles per hour in three seconds, using tires that have 1,600 razor-sharp steel studs that help them grip the ice. The motorcyclists race four at a time in heats that last four laps. The best riders qualify for a final race to determine that day's winner.

AMA SuperBike Racing

These motorcycles fly around the track. The drivers exceed speeds of 190 miles per hour when they compete in 20 races each year at 10 U.S. tracks, including the famed Daytona Speedway.

Tail

The superbike's tail section is made from lightweight fiberglass and is formed to lessen drag.

Racing Suit

Riders wear leather bodysuits that have humps on the back to make them more aerodynamic.

Windshield

The curved Plexiglas channels air away to create a pocket of calm air for the rider's head.

Kneepads

Riders wear pads on each knee so they can really lean in to curves to turn at high speed.

FREESTYLE

High-Octane Acrobats

Freestyle motocross riders defy gravity. They hit a ramp while going 50 miles per hour to launch themselves and their 220-pound bikes more than 60 feet to a dirt ramp they hope to coast down safely. As if that weren't crazy enough, they flip, turn, twist, and let go of their bikes as they fly, performing death-defying tricks like trapeze artists without the net. These three riders show off daring tricks: *(Clockwise)* Ed Rossi lets go of the bike in midair for the "Rock Solid"; Mark Merrix performs the "Shaolin Bar Hop"; and Mike Kieper gets full extension on his "Superman Seat Grab."

SKATE

In the 1950s, a group of California surfers decided to take their favorite pastime to dry land. They grabbed some boards, slapped roller-skate wheels on them, and skateboards were born. At first, these skateboarders just surfed the sidewalks and raced downhill. But in the 1970s, when equipment started to get better, these sidewalk surfers became stylists who did technical tricks like aerials and grinds. It was a group of young skateboarders from Venice Beach and Santa Monica, California, called the Z-Boys, who revolutionized the sport. In 1975, at skateboarding's first national championships, the Z-Boys wowed the crowds. Today, athletes from all over the world — like three-time X Games gold medalist Sandro Dias *(above)* of Brazil — compete in the sport.

HANDS OFF

How does a skateboarder fly through the air while the board seems to stay glued to his or her feet? Science helps explain. When a skateboarder does an "ollie," they push down on the back of the board with one foot. This causes the front of the board to shoot up. If they quickly push down with the front foot, it causes the back of the board to pop up too, helping it stay attached to the rider's feet in the air.

Pool Party

A massive drought in Southern California in the 1970s meant a lot of people in Los Angeles couldn't fill their pools anymore. A crew of young surfers and skaters, the Z-Boys, would scout out empty pools and turn them into impromptu skate parks. The tricks they did in the bowls changed skateboarding. Skate parks would later build ramps that mimicked the shape of those old dried-out cement ponds.

TOM SCHAAR

When he was a 12-year-old sixth-grader, Tom Schaar, a skateboarder from Malibu, California, did something that made the legendary Tony Hawk take notice. Hawk — who earned his crowning achievement at the 1999 X Games, when he became the first person to nail a 900 — finally saw someone achieve three full rotations, a 1080. Who finally did it? Schaar, who hadn't even been born when Hawk nailed his historic trick. Hawk was among the first to know Schaar had done it. Then, when video of the trick came out, he shared it with the masses. But the skateboarding prodigy did not let up after the feat. When he traveled to X Games Asia, he took home gold in the Mini Mega Ramp. At only 13, we may be watching Schaar rewrite the record books for years to come.

The Prodigy

Schaar began skateboarding at the young age of 3 after watching his older brother do it. He felt drawn to vert, because he loved flying through the air off a ramp. At 9 years old, he could land 540s, and at 10, he graduated to 720s. Big-time riders like Hawk and Bob Burnquist knew about his skill, but the whole world took notice after Schaar became the first to nail the 1080.

Ramp It Up!

Some of the most high-flying fun in skateboarding happens on the vert ramp. The first one was actually some 24-foot-wide pipes that were being installed in the Arizona desert for a huge public works project. Skateboarders loved the tricks they could do so much that they started building their own pipes in California, creating a new skateboarding discipline.

During his first year as a pro as an 11-year-old on the Dew Tour, Schaar was already performing difficult tricks like the stalefish, which has become one of his signature moves.

These kids were born to ride, jetting around on Razor scooters at Venice Beach Park in California.

WILD WOODY

Branson, Missouri, is a city filled with theme parks, theaters, museums, and all sorts of other tourist attractions. One of the coolest is a four-story wooden go-kart track called Wild Woody. In one- or two-person go-karts, you'll descend on an all-wood spiral that feels like an oversized roller coaster. Built in 2002 at The Track, Wild Woody gives you 1,440 feet of racing fun. At the park, you can also test your driving skills on a variety of courses, including a 275-foot banked oval to take you to top speed. Or see how nimble you are at steering on the twisting, turning road course track.

All-Access

Want to go where roads don't? That's where all-terrain vehicles come in handy. A lot of outdoorsmen get to their favorite fishing hole or campsite with a little help from their ATVs. These versatile four-wheelers can crawl over rocks, plow through dirt, and even splash through shallow creeks. The first ATVs were made by Honda in 1970 and cost $595. You'll spend more than 10 times that amount if you buy one today, but what you'll get is a four-wheel-drive vehicle that can carry a few hundred pounds and go up to 40 miles per hour.

RECYCLE YOUR WHEELS

Smooth Operators

During a hockey game, players' skates make the ice surface choppy and rough. To get it back in pristine shape, the ice needs to be resurfaced, and that's usually done with a Zamboni machine. Workers fit a Zamboni with studded tires *(above, left)* to give it traction on the ice so that they're ready to go during big events like the NHL Winter Classic at Fenway Park *(above, right)*. The Zamboni functions by shaving off a thin layer of ice, which is then gathered in the snow tank at the front end of the vehicle. Water is sprayed on the ice and then squeegeed and vacuumed off. For the last step, clean water is poured onto the ice and spread evenly. It eventually freezes into a smooth layer of new ice.

Segway riders cruise down a boardwalk.

What kid wouldn't want to go to school if they could get there in Monty Perrigo's monster school bus?